17.

To parents and teachers

We hope you and the children will enjoy reading this story in either English or French. The story is simple, but not *simplified* so the language of the French and the English is quite natural but there is lots of repetition.

At the back of the book is a small picture dictionary with the key words and how to pronounce them. There is also a simple pronunciation guide to the whole story on the last page.

Here are a few suggestions on using the book:

• Read the story aloud in English first, to get to know it. Treat it like any other picture book: look at the pictures, talk about the story and the characters and so on.

• Then look at the picture dictionary and say the French names for the key words. Ask the children to repeat them. Concentrate on speaking the words out loud, rather than reading them.

• Go back and read the story again, this time in English *and* French. Don't worry if your pronunciation isn't quite correct. Just have fun trying it out. Check the guide at the back of the book, if necessary, but you'll soon pick up how to say the French words.

• When you think you and the children are ready, you can try reading the story in French only. Ask the children to say it with you. Only ask them to read it if they are keen to try. The spelling could be confusing and put them off.

• Above all encourage the children to have a go and give lots of praise. Little children are usually quite unselfconscious and this is excellent for building up confidence in a foreign language.

Published by b small publishing
The Book Shed, 36 Leyborne Park, Kew, Richmond, Surrey, TW9 3HA, UK
www.bsmall.co.uk
© b small publishing, 2000
2 3 4 5
All rights reserved.
Printed in China by WKT Company Ltd.

ISBN-13: 978-1-905710-11-9   ISBN-10: 1-905710-11-9 (UK paperback with spine)

Puppy finds a friend

Le petit chien
se trouve un ami

Catherine Bruzzone

Pictures by John Bendall-Brunello
French by Christophe Dillinger

b small publishing

Puppy wakes up.

Le petit chien se réveille.

It's Saturday.

C'est samedi.

"Hmm…who can I play with today?"

"Mmmmm…avec qui je peux jouer aujourd'hui?"

"I'm too tired," says the cat,

"Je suis trop fatigué," dit le chat,

"come back tomorrow."

"reviens demain."

"I'm too busy," says the cow,

"Je suis trop occupée," dit la vache,

"come back later."

"reviens plus tard."

"I'm too hungry," says the horse,

"J'ai trop faim," dit le cheval,

"come back this evening."

"reviens ce soir."

"I can't leave my nest," says the hen,

"Je ne peux pas quitter mon nid,"
                        dit la poule,

"come back on Monday."

"reviens lundi."

"Come and swim with us", says the duck.

"Viens nager avec nous", dit le canard.

But Puppy doesn't like water.

Mais le petit chien n'aime pas l'eau.

So he goes home.
Alors, il rentre à la maison.

He plays with his ball.
Il joue avec sa balle.

He eats his lunch.
Il mange son déjeuner.

He sleeps in his basket.
Il dort dans son panier.

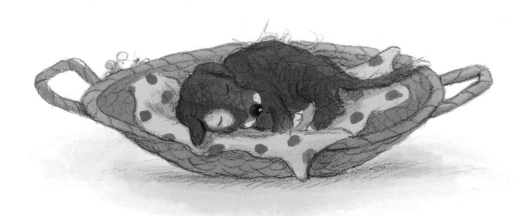

Who's that?

Qui est là?

"Can I play with you, Puppy?"

"Je peux jouer avec toi, petit chien?"

"Mouse, you're my best friend!"

"Souris, tu es ma meilleure amie!"

Pronouncing French

Don't worry if your pronunciation isn't quite correct.
The important thing is to be willing to try. The pronunciation guide here will help but it cannot be completely accurate:

- Read the guide as naturally as possible, as if it were standard British English.

- Put stress on the letters in *italics*, e.g. kan*ar*.

- Don't roll the r at the end of the word, for example in the French word **le** (the): ler.

If you can, ask a French person to help and move on as soon as possible to speaking the words without the guide.

Note French adjectives usually have two forms, one for masculine and one for feminine nouns, e.g. **fatigué** and **fatiguée.**

Words Les Mots

leh moh

cat
le chat

ler shah

duck
le canard

ler kan*ar*

hen
la poule

lah pool

horse
le cheval

ler sh-*val*

cow
la vache

lah vash

puppy
le petit chien

ler p'tee shee-*yah*

mouse
la souris

lah soo*ree*

friend
l'ami/l'amie

lam*ee*/lam*ee*

basket
le panier

ler *pan*-yeh

nest
le nid

ler nee

tired
fatigué/
fatiguée

fatee-*geh*/fatee-*geh*

busy
occupé/
occupée

oh-kew*peh*/oh-kew*peh*

to be hungry
avoir faim

*av*wah fah

ball
la balle

lah bal

lunch
le déjeuner

ler deh-sher*neh*

water
l'eau

loh

to swim
nager

nah-sheh

to play
jouer

shoo-eh

to eat
manger

*mon*sheh

today
aujourd'hui

o'shoor-*dwee*

this evening
ce soir

ser swah

tomorrow
demain

d'*mah*

Monday
lundi

lern-*dee*

Saturday
samedi

sam'*dee*

A simple guide to pronouncing this French story

Le petit chien se trouve un ami
ler p'tee shee-*yah* ser troov ahn am*ee*

Le petit chien se réveille.
ler p'tee shee-*yah* ser reh*vay*

C'est samedi.
seh sam'*dee*

"Mmmmm... avec qui je peux jouer aujourd'hui?"
mmm... avek kee sh' per
shoo-eh o'shoor-*dwee*

"Je suis trop fatigué," dit le chat,
sh' swee troh fatee-*geh*, dee ler shah

"reviens demain."
rer-vee*ah* d'*mah*

Je suis trop occupée," dit la vache,
sh' swee troh oh-kew*peh*, dee la vash

"reviens plus tard."
rer-vee*ah* ploo tar

"J'ai trop faim," dit le cheval,
shay troh fah, dee ler sh-*val*

"reviens ce soir."
rer-vee*ah* ser swah

"Je ne peux pas quitter mon nid," dit la poule,
sh' ner per pah *kee*teh moh nee,
dee lah pool

"reviens lundi."
rer-vee*ah* *lern*-dee

"Viens nager avec nous", dit le canard.
vee*ah* *nah*-sheh avek noo,
dee ler kan*ar*

Mais le petit chien n'aime pas l'eau.
meh ler p'tee shee-*yah* nem pah loh

Alors, il rentre à la maison.
alor, eel rontr' ah lah *meh*-soh

Il joue avec sa balle.
eel shoo avek sah bal

Il mange son déjeuner.
eel monsh' soh deh-sher*neh*

Il dort dans son panier.
eel dor doh soh *pan*-yeh

Qui est là?
kee eh lah

"Je peux jouer avec toi, petit chien?"
sh' per *shoo*-eh avek twah,
p'tee shee-*yah*

"Souris, tu es ma meilleure amie!"
soo*ree*, too eh mah *may*-er am*ee*